THE HUMAN BODY IN FOCUS

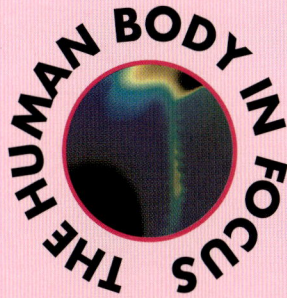

HOW WE DIGEST FOOD

NICOLA BARBER

Adapted from an original text by Carol Ballard

W
FRANKLIN WATTS
LONDON · SYDNEY

First published in 2009 by Franklin Watts

Copyright © 2009 Arcturus Publishing Limited

Franklin Watts
338 Euston Road
London NW1 3BH

Franklin Watts Australia
Level 17/207 Kent Street, Sydney, NSW 2000

Produced by Arcturus Publishing Limited,
26/27 Bickels Yard, 151–153 Bermondsey Street, London SE1 3HA

The right of Nicola Barber to be identified as the author of this work has been asserted by her in accordance with the Copyright, Designs and Patents Act 1988.

Understanding the Human Body is based on the series *Exploring the Human Body*, published by Franklin Watts.

Editor: Alex Woolf
Designer: Peta Phipps and Mike Reynolds
Illustrator: Michael Courtney
Picture researcher: Glass Onion Pictures
Consultant: Dr Kristina Routh

Picture Credits
Science Photo Library: 5 (Bluestone), 7 (Lauren Shear), 9 (Mark Clarke), 11 (BSIP, Laurent), 13 (Eye of Science), 15 (Eye of Science), 17 (Coneyl Jay), 19 (Ian Boddy), 20 (Maximilian Stock Ltd), 21 (Mark Clarke), 22 (Ricardo Arias, Latin Stock), 24 (Jason Kelvin), 25 (BSIP, Chassenet), 26 (Jim Gipe/Agstock), 27 (Adrienne Hart-Davis), 28 (Adam Hart-Davis), 29 (Bluestone).
Shutterstock: cover (Anton Albert).

Every attempt has been made to clear copyright. Should there be any inadvertent omission, please apply to the publisher for rectification.

A CIP catalogue record for this book is available from the British Library.

Dewey Decimal Classification Number: 612.3

ISBN 978 0 7496 9058 8

Printed in China

Franklin Watts is a division of Hachette Children's Books, an Hachette UK Company
www.hachette.co.uk

Contents

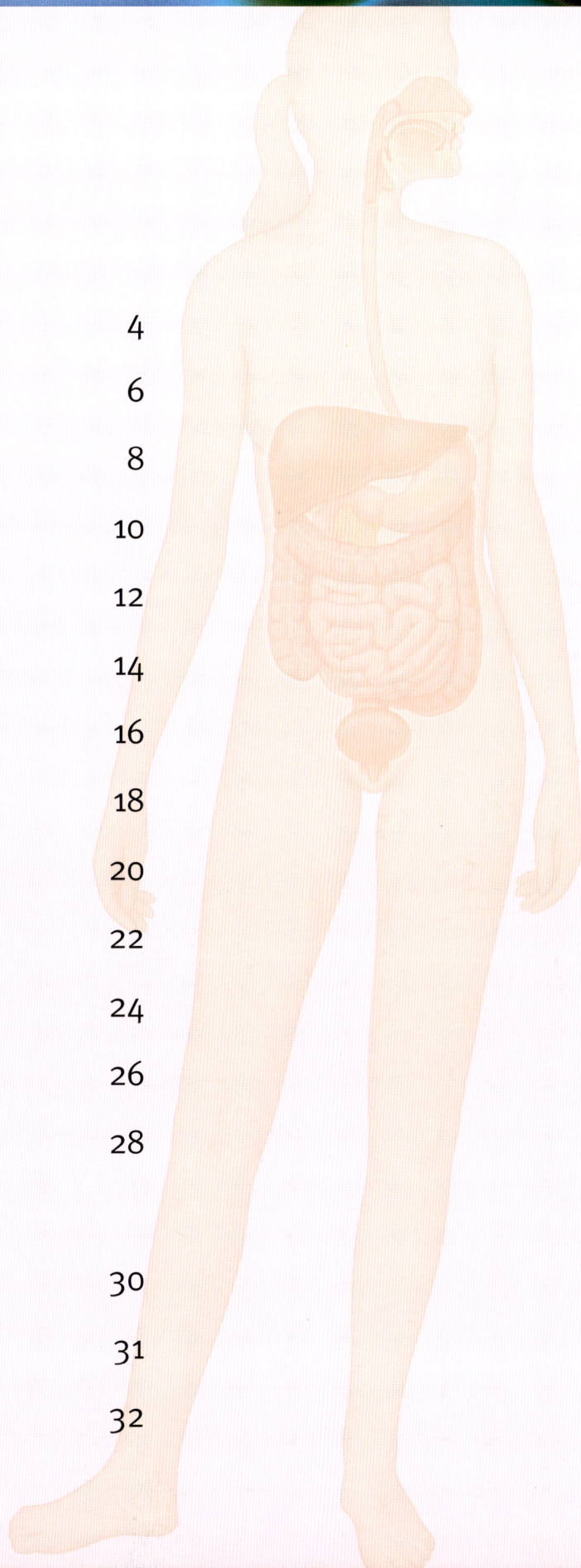

What is
Digestion?

Food provides everything you need to grow and to stay healthy. But your body cannot use the food just as it is. As you eat, your body breaks the food down into different substances. This process is called **digestion**.

Digestive system

Your body is made up of many different parts. Each part has its own special job to do. Digestion is carried out by the various parts of your **digestive system**. All the parts work together to break down your food as it passes through.

This picture shows your digestive system inside your body.

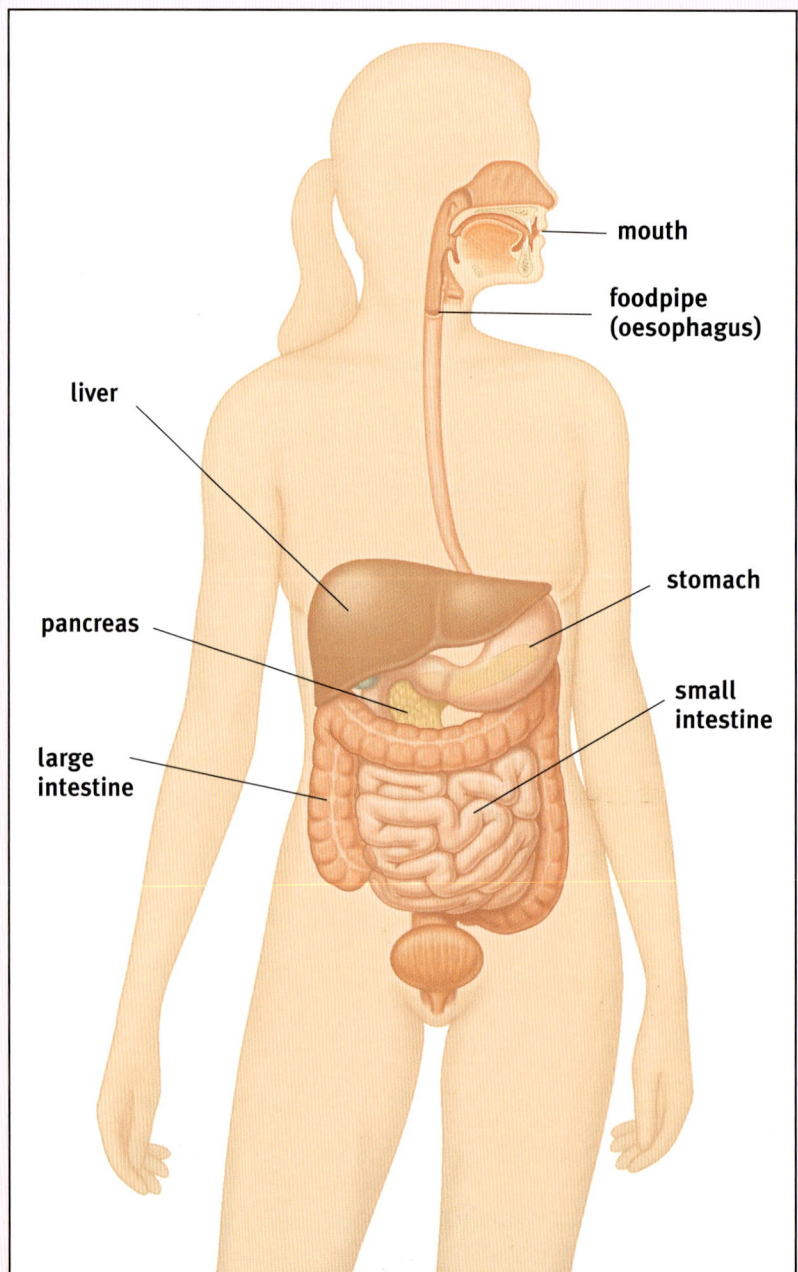

mouth

foodpipe (oesophagus)

liver

pancreas

stomach

small intestine

large intestine

Digestion begins in your mouth. You chew a mouthful of food and swallow it. When you swallow, the chewed-up food passes into the foodpipe (oesophagus). From there, it moves into the stomach. It passes into the **small intestine** and on into the **large intestine**. When there are no useful substances left, the waste leaves your body. This is when you go to the toilet.

An apple is a delicious and healthy snack.

Q&A

Why do we need food?

Food provides your body with the substances it needs for:

1. Energy for activity. Even when you are asleep, your body uses energy as you breathe.

2. Making new skin, bone, muscle and other things. Your body needs to be able to grow, and to repair damage if you cut your knee or break your arm.

3. Staying healthy. Your body needs substances from food to help it fight infection and disease.

Essential jobs

Other parts of your body are involved in digestion, too. Although they are not part of the digestive system, they carry out essential jobs. They include your **liver, pancreas, kidneys** and **bladder**.

Teeth

You use your teeth to bite, tear and chew food. Each of these jobs is done by different teeth.

Incisor teeth are at the front of your mouth. They have sharp edges for biting into food. **Canine** teeth are the pointed teeth on each side of the incisors. They are good for gripping and tearing food. Premolar teeth are behind the canines. They have blunt, broad surfaces for crushing food. **Molar** teeth are at the back of your mouth. Their large, bumpy surfaces are ideal for chewing and mashing food.

Inside a tooth

You only see part of each tooth. This part is called the crown. The rest is stuck firmly inside your jawbone. Teeth have several layers.

This diagram shows the layers that make up a tooth.

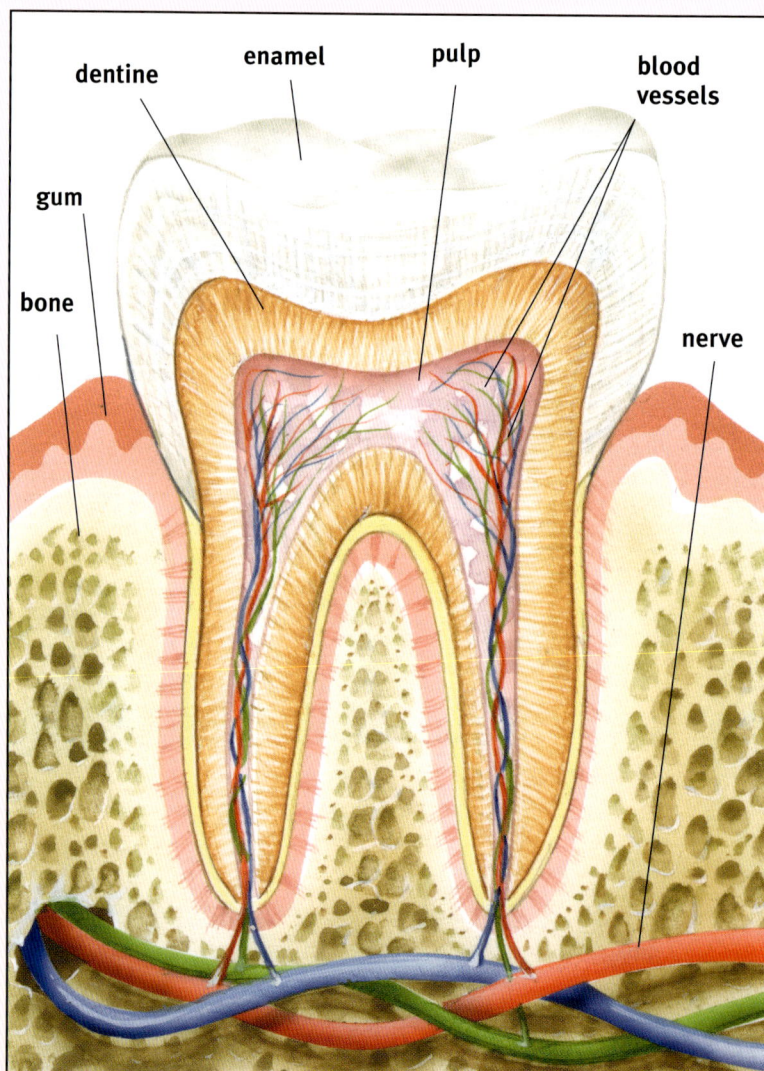

The outer layer of enamel is hard and shiny. Underneath is a hard layer called dentine. The soft centre of a tooth is called pulp. It contains **nerves** and **blood vessels**.

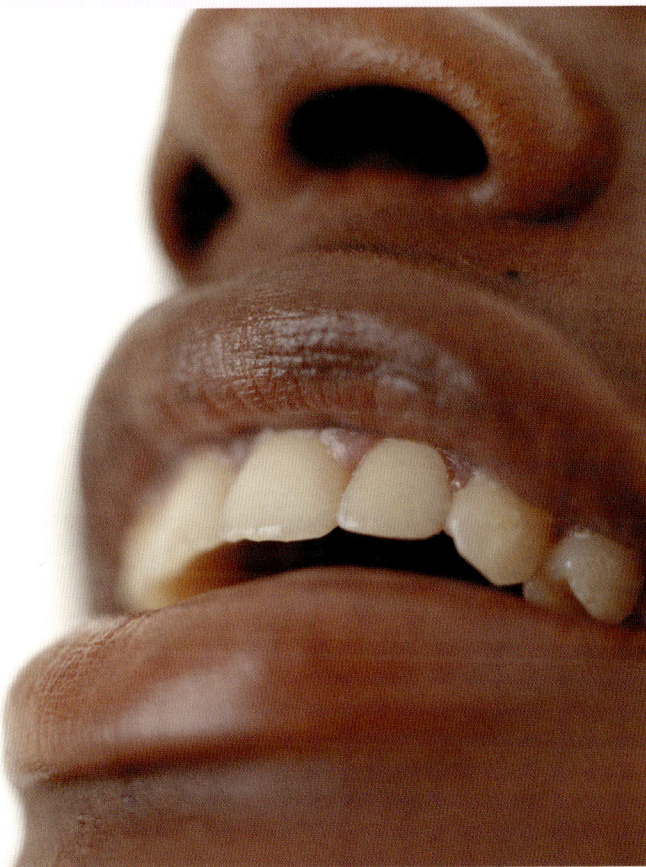

Here you can see the different types of front teeth.

Milk teeth

Babies are born without any teeth. By the time they are about three years old, they have a set of 20 'milk teeth'. Between about six and 12 years old, the milk teeth fall out. New teeth grow in their place. These are the teeth you have for the rest of your life.

Q&A

How many teeth do adults have?

Adults have 32 teeth. There are eight incisors, four canines, eight premolars and 12 molars. The final four molars are called wisdom teeth. They do not usually appear until several years after the other molars. Sometimes they do not appear at all.

Mouth

When you take a bite of food, your teeth crush it into small, soft pieces. The pieces are mixed with a liquid called **saliva**. The saliva comes from **glands** under your tongue and the sides of your mouth. Saliva makes the food moist and slippery so that it is easy to swallow.

Taste buds

Your tongue moves your food around inside your mouth. The top of your tongue has special cells called **taste buds**. When food touches the taste buds, they send signals to your brain. There are only four main tastes – sweet, salty, bitter and sour. These four tastes mix together to make all the flavours that we enjoy in our food.

This diagram shows the inside of your mouth.

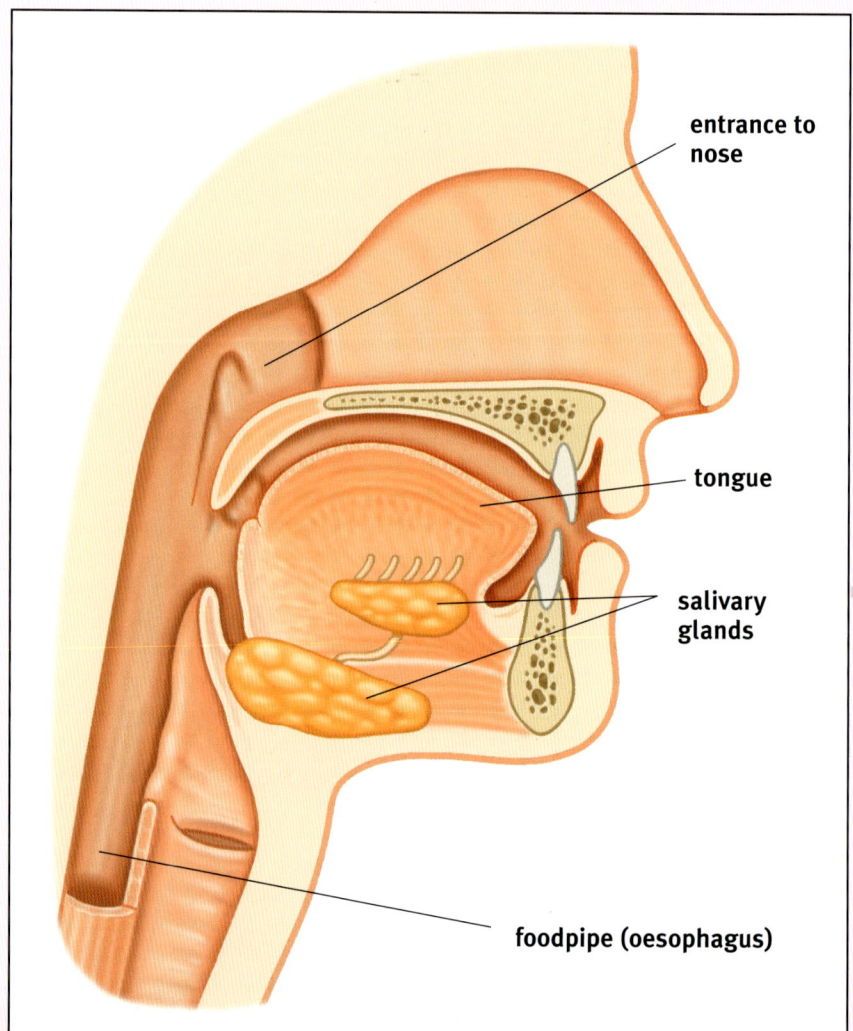

entrance to nose

tongue

salivary glands

foodpipe (oesophagus)

Which flavours do you like best?

To the stomach

When you swallow, the food goes into your foodpipe, or oesophagus. The oesophagus is a tube that connects your mouth and **stomach**. Muscles in the tube walls move in waves to force the food towards the stomach. Most of the time a ring of muscle keeps the entrance to the stomach closed. When food reaches the entrance, the ring opens to let the food through.

Q&A

What happens when I vomit?

Sometimes you have to get rid of whatever is in your stomach. To do this, the ring of muscle at the top of the stomach opens. The muscles force food into the oesophagus. The oesophagus muscles push the food backwards and out through the mouth. We call this being sick, or vomiting. The vomit tastes horrible. This is because the food has been mixed with acid and other juices in your stomach.

Stomach

Your **stomach** is at the end of your oesophagus, just below your ribs. It is like a balloon with a stretchy outside and a space inside. The wall of the stomach is made of strong, elastic muscles. When these muscles stretch, the space inside becomes big enough to contain a whole meal!

Stomach walls

The stomach wall has several layers. There is an outer layer, then layers of muscles, and then a wrinkly inner lining. The lining of the stomach contains special **glands**. These glands make a liquid called gastric juice. This liquid is a mixture of chemicals that break down the food.

This diagram shows what your stomach is like inside.

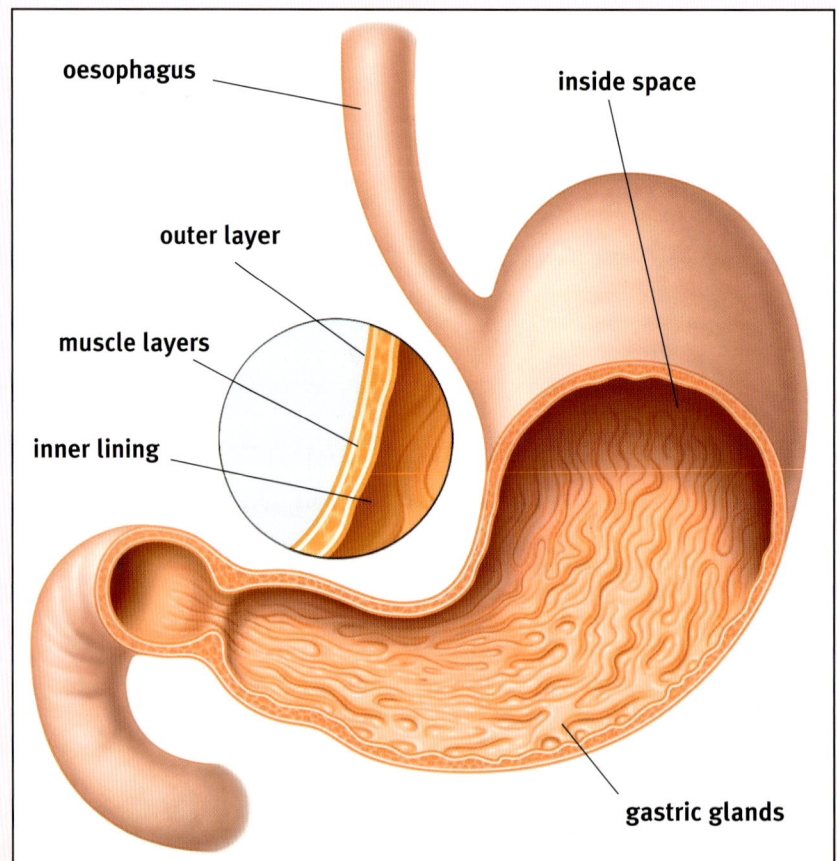

oesophagus

inside space

outer layer

muscle layers

inner lining

gastric glands

You may feel uncomfortable after a big meal, but a quiet rest will often help you to feel better

Q&A

What causes indigestion?

Sometimes, after a meal, you may have a tummy ache or feel sick. This is called indigestion. Several things can cause it:

• some types of food

• eating too much

• eating too quickly

• stress

Indigestion may be uncomfortable but it soon passes and it is not dangerous.

Chyme

When food enters the stomach, the muscles of the stomach wall begin to shorten and lengthen. These muscle movements churn the food around so that it mixes with the gastric juices. Slowly, the food turns into a thick liquid called chyme. When the chyme is ready to leave the stomach, a ring of muscle at the lower end opens. Chyme squirts out of the stomach and into the next part of the **digestive system**, the **small intestine**.

Small Intestine

The **small intestine** is actually the longest part of the **digestive system**. If it was fully stretched out, it would be more than six metres long! It is called 'small' because it is a very narrow tube. It is coiled up tightly so that it can fit inside your abdomen.

Digestion

The walls of the small intestine are made up of layers, like the stomach wall. The layers of muscles move like a wave to push the chyme along. The inner lining contains **glands** that make a slippery liquid called mucus. This helps the chyme to slide along smoothly. Digestive juices that contain special chemicals called **enzymes** break down the food completely.

Chemicals called enzymes break down food into nutrients that your body can use.

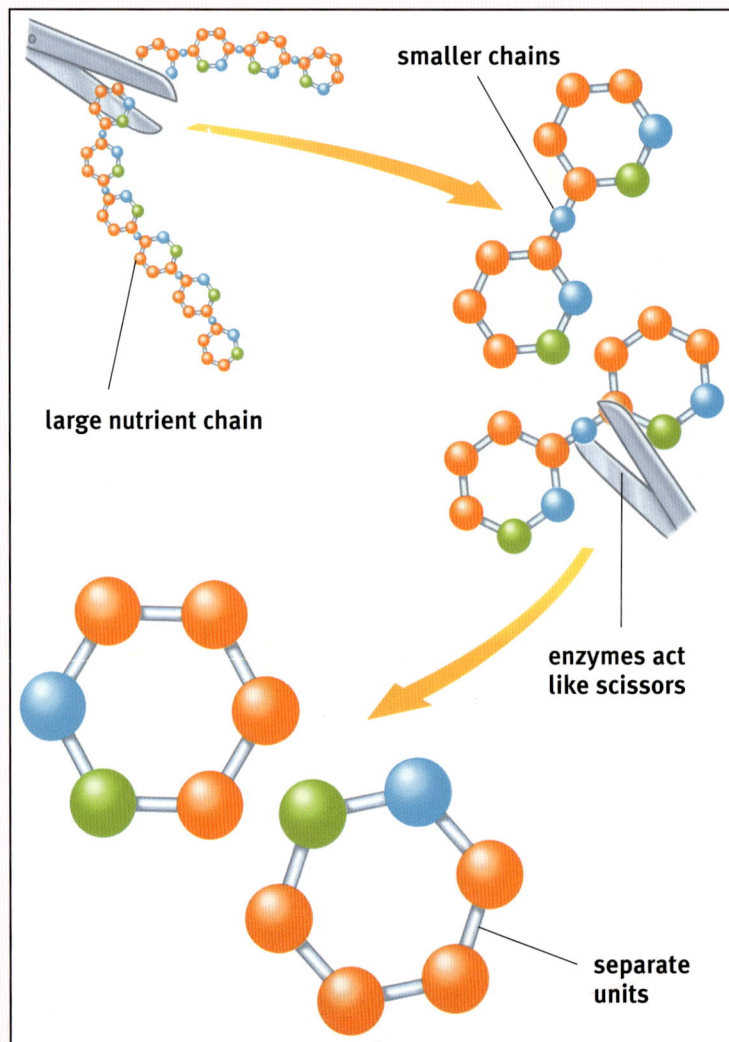

smaller chains

large nutrient chain

enzymes act like scissors

separate units

Villi

The inner lining of the small intestine has millions of tiny fingers called villi. The villi have **blood vessels** inside them. **Nutrients** from the food pass through the walls of the villi. The nutrients go into the blood. They are then carried away to other parts of the body.

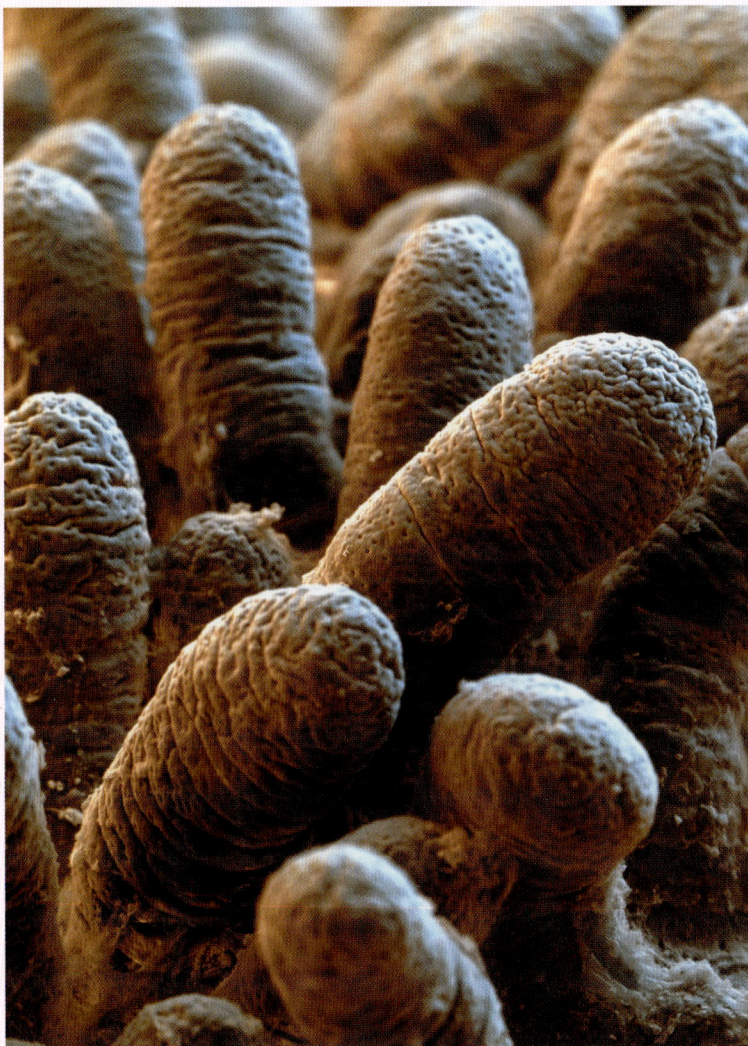

This photograph was taken with a microscope. You can see the villi on the inside lining of the small intestine.

Q&A

Why can't some people drink milk?

Milk contains a type of sugar called lactose. Lactose is usually broken down in the small intestine by a chemical called lactase. Some people do not produce enough lactase in the small intestine. This means the lactose will not break down. It stays in the waste, causing **diarrhoea,** wind and cramps.

By the time it reaches the end of the small intestine, the food is completely digested. All that is left is waste material your body cannot use.

Large Intestine

After passing through the **small intestine,** the food goes into the **large intestine**. The large intestine is about a metre long. It is much wider than the small intestine. It bends round to make a rectangular shape around the small intestine. Its walls are made up of layers, just like the stomach and small intestine.

Parts of the intestine

The first part of the large intestine is called the caecum. Attached to the caecum is a long, thin pouch called the appendix. The main part of the large intestine is called the colon. The muscles in the colon walls push the waste along. The colon walls also absorb water from the waste, so the waste becomes drier and more solid.

colon

caecum

appendix

rectum

anus

This diagram shows the parts of your large intestine.

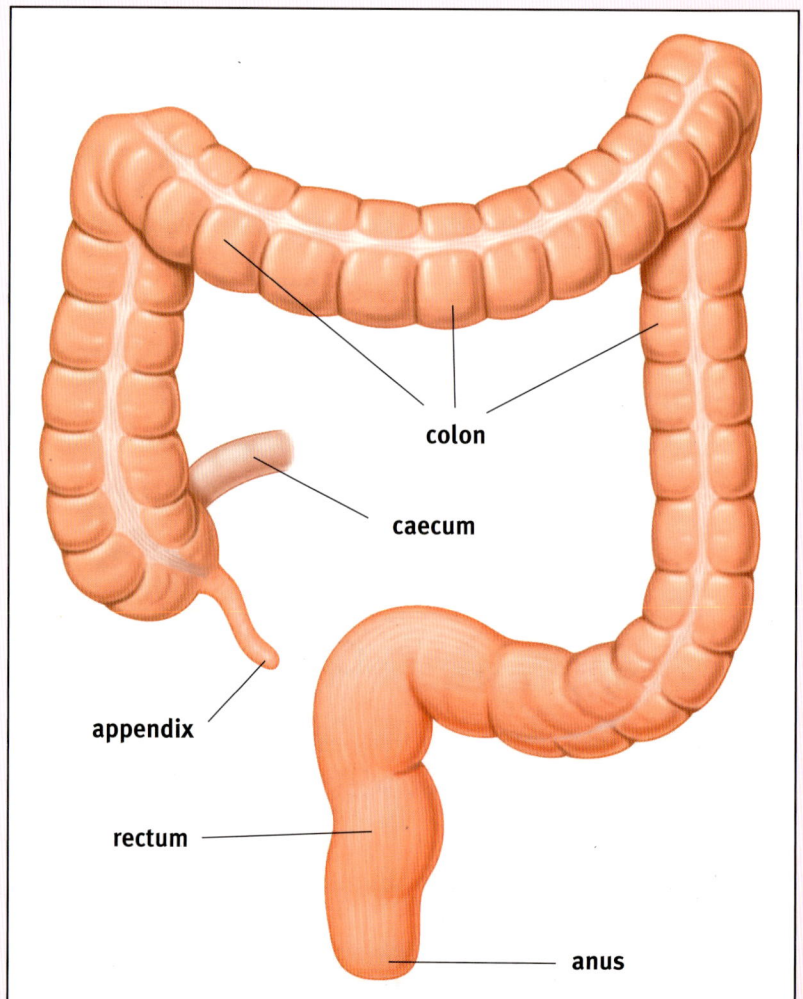

The rectum

The final part of the large intestine is the **rectum**. This is where the solid waste material, called **faeces**, is stored. When the rectum becomes full, you feel you need to go to the toilet. There is a ring of muscle, called the **anus**, around the end of the rectum. When this opens, faeces pass through and leave your body.

Keeping clean

Faeces contain lots of germs. To keep yourself clean and healthy, you should always wash your hands after using the toilet.

Look at the germs that can grow if you do not wash your hands!

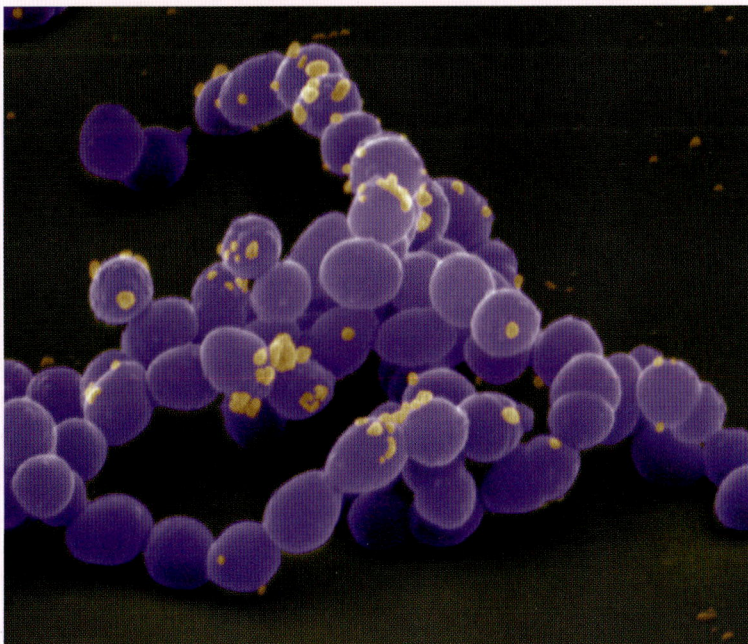

Q&A

How long does food stay in the intestines?

Normally, it takes between six and 15 hours for food to pass right through the intestines. But sometimes your body needs to get rid of food quickly. The food rushes through the intestines much faster than normal. This is called **diarrhoea**. When you go to the toilet, the waste is much softer than usual. This is because there is not enough time for water to be absorbed in the large intestine.

Liver and Pancreas

Food does not pass through the **liver** or **pancreas**. But without them, you would not be able to digest your food properly.

The liver

The liver does lots of jobs. It helps to control the amount of sugar in your blood. It helps break down old blood cells and stores any useful chemicals they contain. It also removes harmful chemicals from your blood.

Bile

One of the liver's important jobs is to produce a liquid called bile. This is stored in a small pouch called the **gall bladder**. The gall bladder releases bile into the **small intestine,** where it breaks down fats.

The pancreas

The pancreas produces pancreatic juice and releases it into the small intestine. Pancreatic juice contains **enzymes** that help to digest food. The pancreas also produces insulin and glucagon. These are chemicals that help to control the amount of sugar in the blood.

The liver is a large organ that lies just below your ribs. The pancreas lies just behind your stomach.

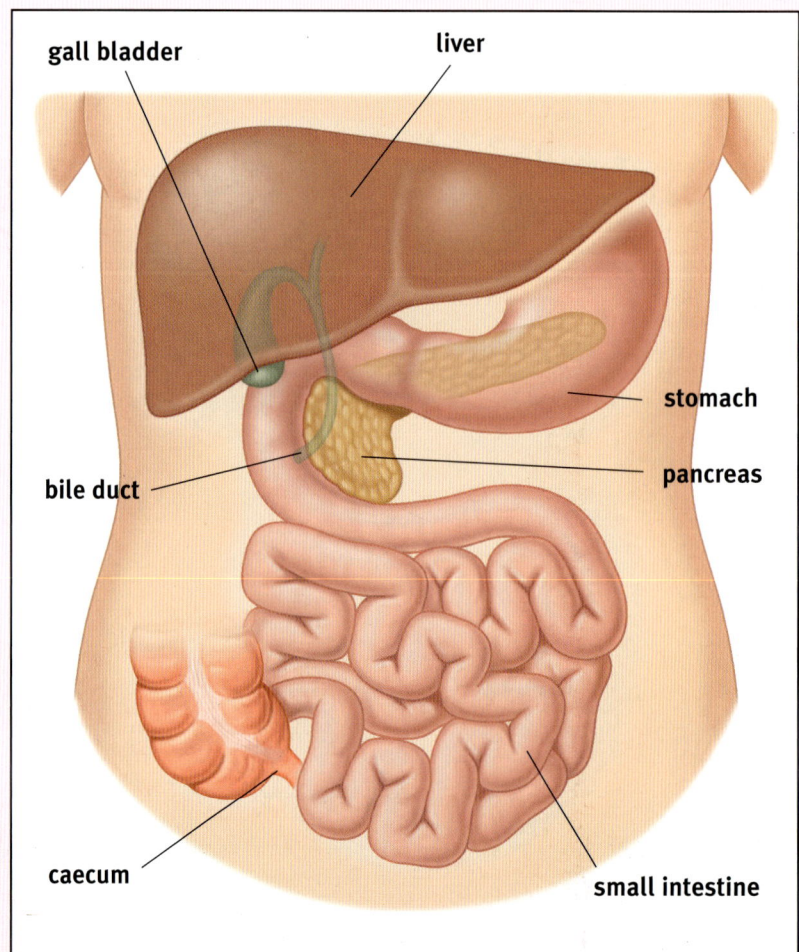

gall bladder

liver

bile duct

stomach

pancreas

caecum

small intestine

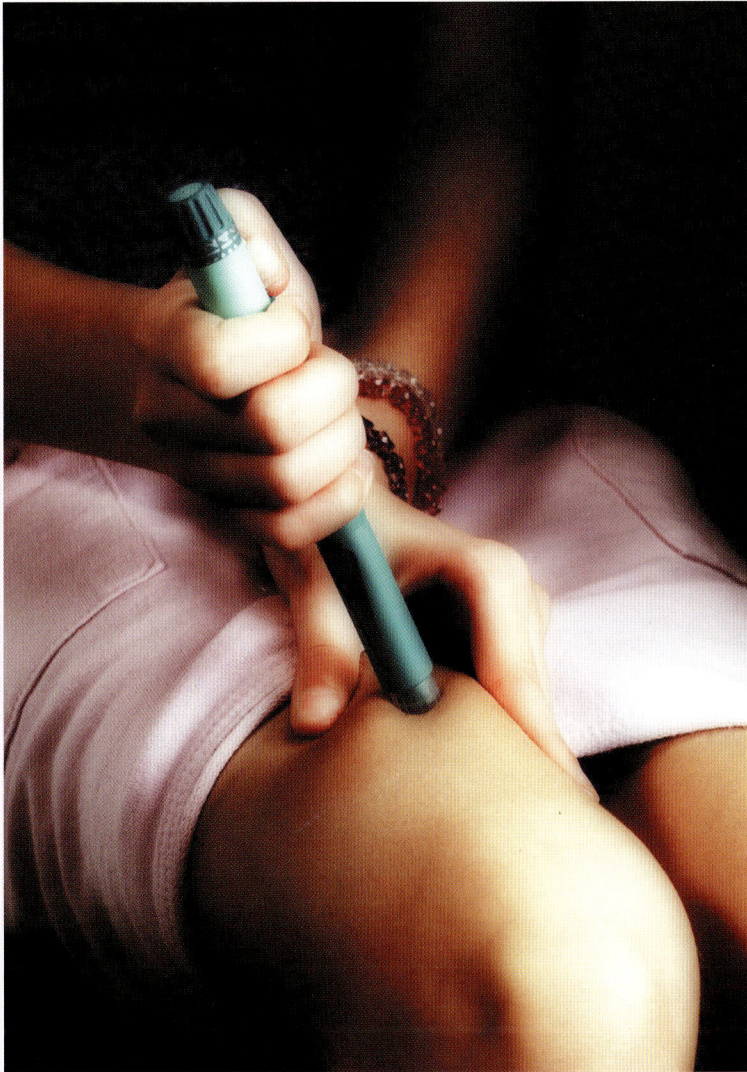

This girl has diabetes. She needs regular injections of insulin.

Working together

The liver and pancreas work together to make sure there is exactly the right amount of sugar in the blood. If there is not enough, the pancreas produces extra glucagon. This makes the liver release sugar into the blood. If there is too much sugar, the pancreas produces extra insulin. This makes the liver take sugar out of the blood.

Q&A

What is diabetes?

People with diabetes cannot control the amount of sugar in the blood. Their pancreas may not produce enough insulin, or their body may not use the insulin properly. People with diabetes must eat a low-sugar diet, exercise regularly and make sure they are not overweight. Some people also need regular injections of insulin.

Kidneys and Bladder

Your blood collects water and **nutrients** from the intestines. It also collects waste products from every part of your body. When blood reaches the **kidneys**, it is full of waste materials that need to be removed.

Filter system

You have two kidneys, one on either side of your spine. Each kidney is about ten centimetres long. Inside a kidney are millions of tiny tubes called nephrons. As blood travels around the nephrons, they filter out some water, salts, **minerals** and other chemicals. Clean blood leaves the kidneys and travels back around to other parts of the body.

Urine

The water and waste materials collect in the centre of the kidney. They make the liquid we call **urine**. The urine leaves the kidney through a tube called the ureter. The ureter takes the urine to the **bladder**.

Here you can see where the kidneys and bladder are in the body.

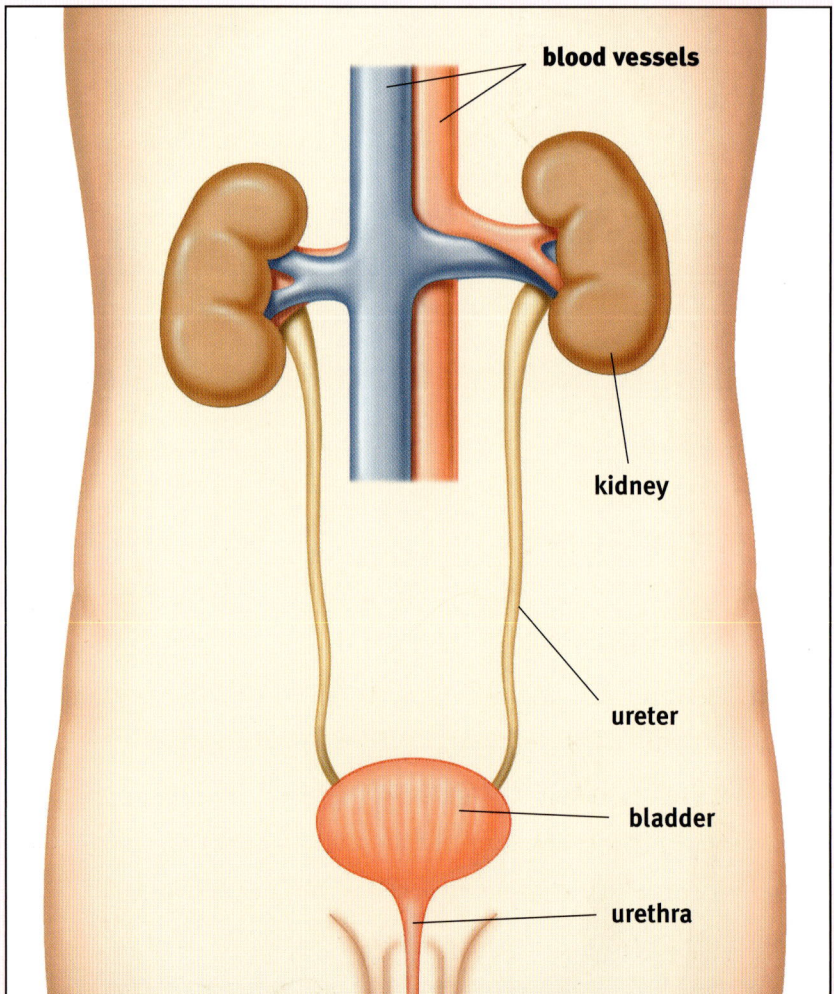

blood vessels

kidney

ureter

bladder

urethra

It is important to wash your hands after using the toilet.

Bladder and urethra

The bladder is a stretchy bag. It slowly fills up with urine from the kidneys. It can hold more than half a litre of urine! When it is nearly full, it sends signals to your brain. Then you know you need to empty your bladder. Urine leaves your body through a tube called the urethra. When you go to the toilet, you open a ring of muscle around the end of the urethra to let the urine flow out.

Q&A

Why is urine yellow?

Urine is mainly water with a lot of chemicals in it. It gets its yellowish colour from a chemical called bilirubin. This is made when old blood cells are broken down by the **liver**. Bilirubin leaves the liver as part of the bile and enters the **digestive system**. From there, it moves into the blood. The kidneys remove the bilirubin from the blood and it goes into your urine.

A **Balanced Diet**

Your diet is everything you eat and drink. Food and liquid provide your body with all the **nutrients** it needs to be active, grow and stay healthy. Different types of food provide different nutrients. A diet that contains all the nutrients you need is called a balanced diet.

There are four main groups of nutrients:
- **proteins**
- **vitamins** and **minerals**
- **carbohydrates**
- fats

A balanced diet includes a wide variety of foods.

Make sure you drink plenty of water, especially when you're very active!

Drinking water

To stay healthy, it is also important to drink plenty of water. This helps your **kidneys** to work well. This is especially important in hot weather, and when you are doing sport.

Fat and thin

The food you eat gives you energy. To stay healthy, you need to balance the amount you eat with the amount of energy you use. If you eat more than your body needs, your body stores the extra as fat. People who are extremely fat are described as obese. Being obese can be very bad for a person's health.

If you eat less than your body needs, your body uses up all of its fat stores. This makes your body weaker and you might feel too tired to be active. Being too thin can be just as bad for your health as being too fat.

Q&A

What is anorexia?

Some people become very unhappy about the way they look. They may stop eating properly. As they eat less and less they become very thin. This makes them weak and ill. This illness is called anorexia. Anorexia is so dangerous that some people die from it.

Proteins

You get **proteins** in foods such as meat, fish, eggs and nuts. Foods made from milk, called dairy products, are also good sources of protein. They include milk, cheese and yoghurt.

Building blocks

Proteins are the building blocks for your body. They help you to grow strong. They also help to repair damage such as cut skin and broken bones. If there is not enough protein in your diet, your body will not be strong and healthy. It is a good idea to try to eat at least two portions of protein-rich food every day.

Meat is a good source of protein.

Amino acids

Proteins are made from chemicals called **amino acids**. The amino acids are strung together, rather like beads on a necklace. When you digest proteins, your body separates the amino acids. Your body then rearranges the amino acids in different orders to make new proteins. This means your body can make all the different proteins it needs.

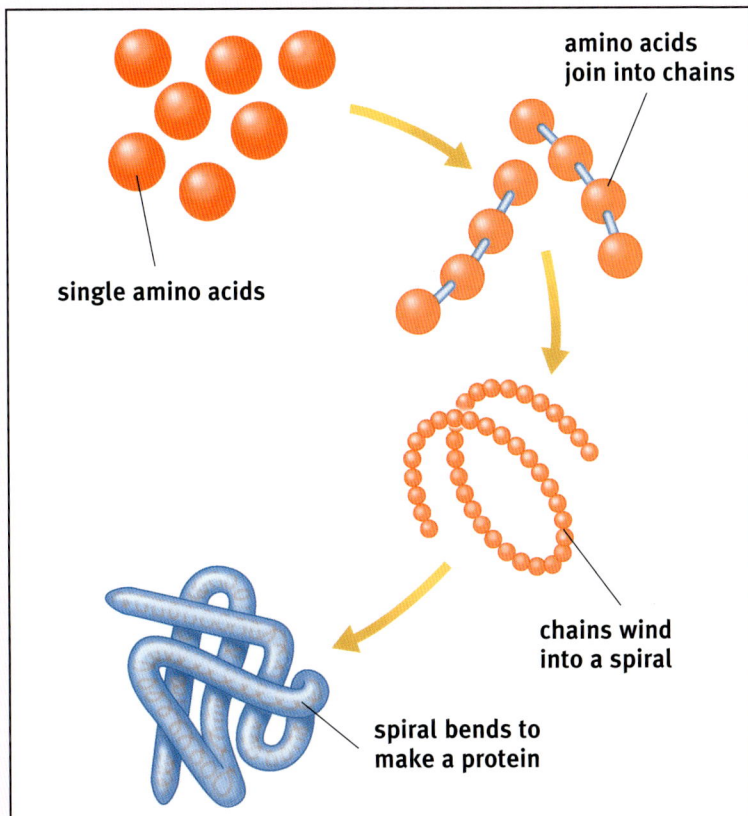

amino acids
join into chains

single amino acids

chains wind
into a spiral

spiral bends to
make a protein

This picture shows how amino acids are put together to make a protein.

Vegetarians

Many people are vegetarians, which means that they do not eat meat. Vegans do not eat any animal products at all. Vegetarians and vegans have to get their proteins from other foods.

Q&A

What if I'm vegetarian?

Being vegetarian is fine – you can be just as strong and healthy as people who eat meat. You need to make sure your diet contains a mixture of different protein-rich foods. These include lentils, pulses, nuts and soya. Cheese and milk are also good protein sources for vegetarians.

Vitamins, Minerals and **Fibre**

Vitamins and **minerals** are essential to keep your body fit and healthy. They are found in many different foods, but mainly in fruits and vegetables. You should try to eat five portions of fresh fruit and vegetables every day.

Vitamins

There are 15 main vitamins. The table below shows some vitamins, the foods that provide them, and why the vitamins are needed:

Eating an orange will give you plenty of vitamin C.

Vitamin	Good sources	Needed for
A	dairy products, eggs and green vegetables	healthy eyes and skin
B (there are several different B vitamins)	wholemeal bread, meat, liver and some beans	healthy skin and general good health
C	citrus fruits and green vegetables	healing cuts and strengthening your body's defences
D	oily fish and dairy products	strong teeth and bones

These dairy products are rich in calcium, which helps to build strong bones and teeth.

Minerals

There are about 20 minerals that are essential to your body. Two of the most important are iron and calcium. Foods that are rich in iron include meat, eggs and leafy green vegetables. Your body needs iron to make a **protein** called haemoglobin. This protein helps to carry oxygen around your body. Calcium is found in dairy products. It is important for bones and teeth. Without calcium, bones become weak and can break easily.

Fibre

You get fibre from fruit and vegetables. Fibre does not contain any **nutrients**, but it is an important part of your diet. Fibre helps food to move easily through the intestines.

Q&A

Can oranges really stop me getting a cold?

Many people eat oranges and drink orange juice to avoid catching colds. Oranges contain a lot of vitamin C. This can help your body to fight off colds and other illnesses.

Carbohydrates

Starches and sugars belong to a group of chemicals called **carbohydrates**. They provide energy and are found in a lot of the foods we eat.

Starches

Foods that contain starch make you feel full. Starchy foods include bread, pasta, rice and cereals. Potatoes are also full of starch. These foods provide energy. Your body digests them slowly, so they help you to feel full for a long time.

Cereals crops like this are ground into flour to make foods such as bread and pasta.

Sweets like these are delicious. But you should try not to eat too many!

Sugars

Sugar makes foods taste sweet. Sugar is used in foods such as cakes, biscuits, sweets and fizzy drinks. A small portion of sugary food gives you a quick burst of energy. But sugary foods and drinks do not satisfy you for very long. It makes sense to think of these foods as a treat. Sugar is also very bad for your teeth. It forms a thin white film called plaque that sticks to your teeth. Plaque can rot your teeth and cause gum disease.

Q&A

Why is wholemeal bread better than white?

Bread is made from cereal grains such as wheat. These grains are full of **vitamins** and fibre. The grains are ground and turned into flour. All of the grain is used to make wholemeal flour. But to make white bread, a lot of the grain is thrown away. This means a lot of the vitamins and fibre are lost.

Fats and Oils

You get fats and oils from fried foods and from dairy products and nuts. Fats and oils provide a lot of energy. They have other important chemicals that your body needs. Fats also help to keep your body warm.

You can check how much fat a food contains by looking at the label.

INGREDIENTS AS SERVED (Greatest first)
Rice, Water, Beef, Prepared Soya Protein, Onion, Cornflour, Red & Green Peppers, Tomato, Sugar, Carrot, Peas, Beef Fat with Antioxidant (BHA), Curry Spices, Salt, Yeast Extract, Citric Acid, Flavour Enhancers (Monosodium Glutamate, Sodium 5'-Ribonucleotide), Colour (Caramel), Maltodextrin, Hydrogenated Vegetable Oil and Acidity Regulator (Sodium Citrate). Less than 10% meat as served.

NUTRITIONAL INFORMATION		
Typical Values	Per 100g as Sold	Per 100g as Served
Energy	1526kJ / 365kcal	458kJ / 109kcal
Protein	11.5g	3.5g
Carbohydrate	63.7g	19.1g
of which Sugars	7.4g	2.2g
Fat	7.1g	2.1g
of which Saturates	3.3g	1.0g
Sodium	1.4g	0.4g
Fibre	5.2g	1.6g

Types of fat

There are two types of fat: saturated and unsaturated. Foods that come from animals have saturated fats. They include dairy products and fatty meat. Foods such as nuts and vegetable oils have unsaturated fats. Many doctors think that unsaturated fats are better for your health than saturated fats. If you eat a lot of animal fats, you may increase your risk of suffering from heart disease.

Biscuits, cakes and sweet popcorn contain a lot of fat.

Low fat

One way to cut down on the amount of fat in your diet is to choose low-fat or fat-free foods. For example, semi-skimmed milk is treated to remove some of the fat. Skimmed milk has almost all of the fat removed. Some food producers make low-fat cakes or biscuits. This means that people can eat foods they enjoy without taking in too much fat.

Q&A

Why are fatty foods linked to heart disease?

Many doctors believe that fatty foods can lead to heart disease. This is because fatty foods contain chemicals that clog up the **blood vessels**. This makes it difficult for blood to get through the vessels. The heart has to pump harder to push the blood around the body.

Glossary

amino acid   One of the tiny units that build proteins.

anus   The opening through which faeces leave the body.

bladder   The organ where urine is stored until you go to the toilet.

blood vessel   One of the tubes through which blood travels around the body.

canine   A pointed tooth at the side of the mouth.

carbohydrate   A type of nutrient that provides energy.

diarrhoea   A condition in which faeces is passed more frequently than usual, and are very soft or even liquid.

digestion   The process of breaking down food into separate chemicals.

digestive system   The organs that together carry out the process of digestion.

enzyme   A chemical that helps chemical changes to take place.

faeces   Solid waste.

gall bladder   A pouch where bile is stored.

gland   A part of your body that releases a particular substance. There are many different types of glands.

incisor   A sharp tooth at the front of the mouth.

kidney   The part of the body that filters the blood. You have two kidneys.

large intestine   The part of the digestive system where water is absorbed.

liver   An organ involved in many chemical changes in the body.

mineral   A substance that is needed in very small quantities to maintain health.

molar   A large, strong tooth at the back of the mouth.

nerve   A part of the body that carries signals to and from the brain.

nutrient   A part of your food that your body can use.

pancreas   The organ that produces insulin and glucagon.

protein   A nutrient that is needed for growth and repair.

rectum   The end of the large intestine, where faeces are stored until you go to the toilet.

saliva   A liquid that softens food in the mouth.

small intestine   The part of the digestive system where nutrients are absorbed.

stomach   The organ where food is broken down into chyme.

taste bud   One of the special cells on your tongue that allows you to taste food.

urine   Liquid waste.

vitamin   A substance needed in very small quantities to maintain health.

Further Information

Books

Body Science: Digesting Food
by Richard Walker (Franklin Watts, 2004)
Kingfisher Knowledge: Human Body
by Richard Walker (Kingfisher, 2006)
Our Bodies: Digestion
by Steve Parker (Wayland, 2004)
The Oxford Children's A to Z of the Human Body
by Bridget and Neil Ardley (Oxford University Press, 2003)
Under the Microscope: Digesting
by Angela Royston (Franklin Watts, 2001)
Usborne Internet-Linked Complete Book of the Human Body
by Anna Claybourne (Usborne Publishing, 2003)

Websites

www.innerbody.com (click on picture of digestive system)
kidshealth.org/kid/htbw/digestive_system.html
www.kidshealth.org/teen/nutrition
www.bbc.co.uk/science/humanbody/body/factfiles/stomach/stomach.shtml

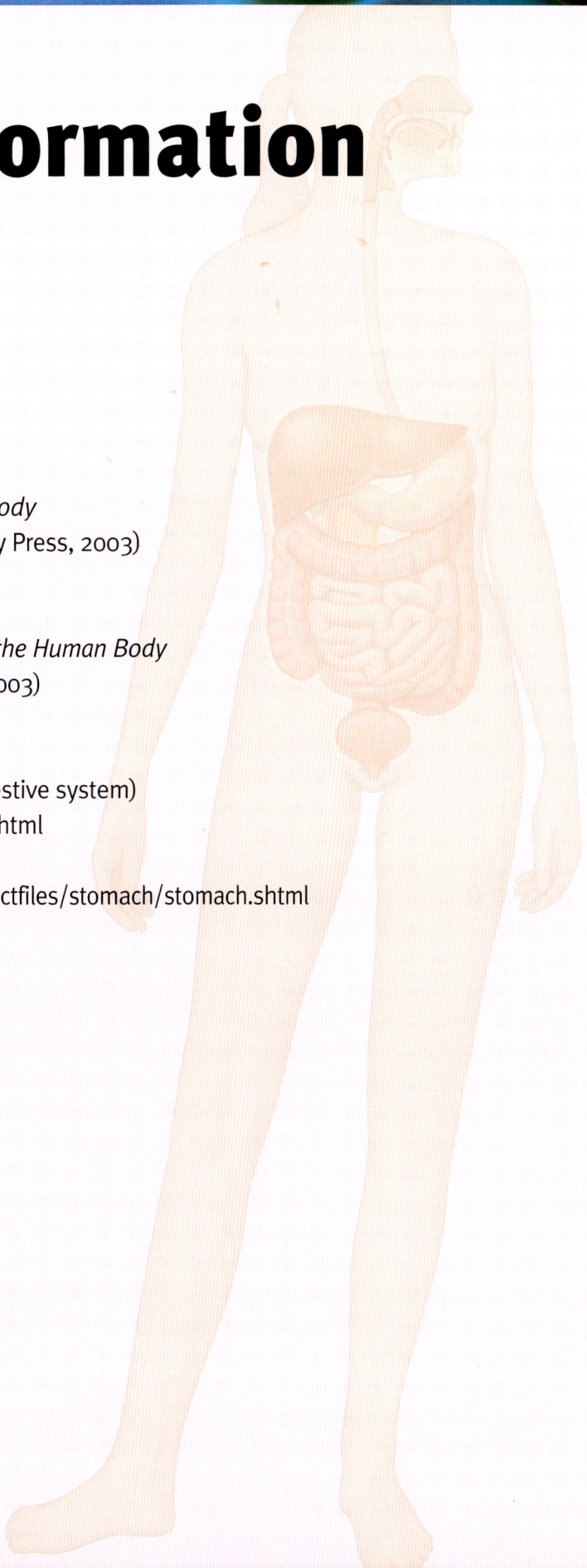

Index

Page numbers in **bold** refer to illustrations.